THE FIRST GOLDEN GEOGRAPHY

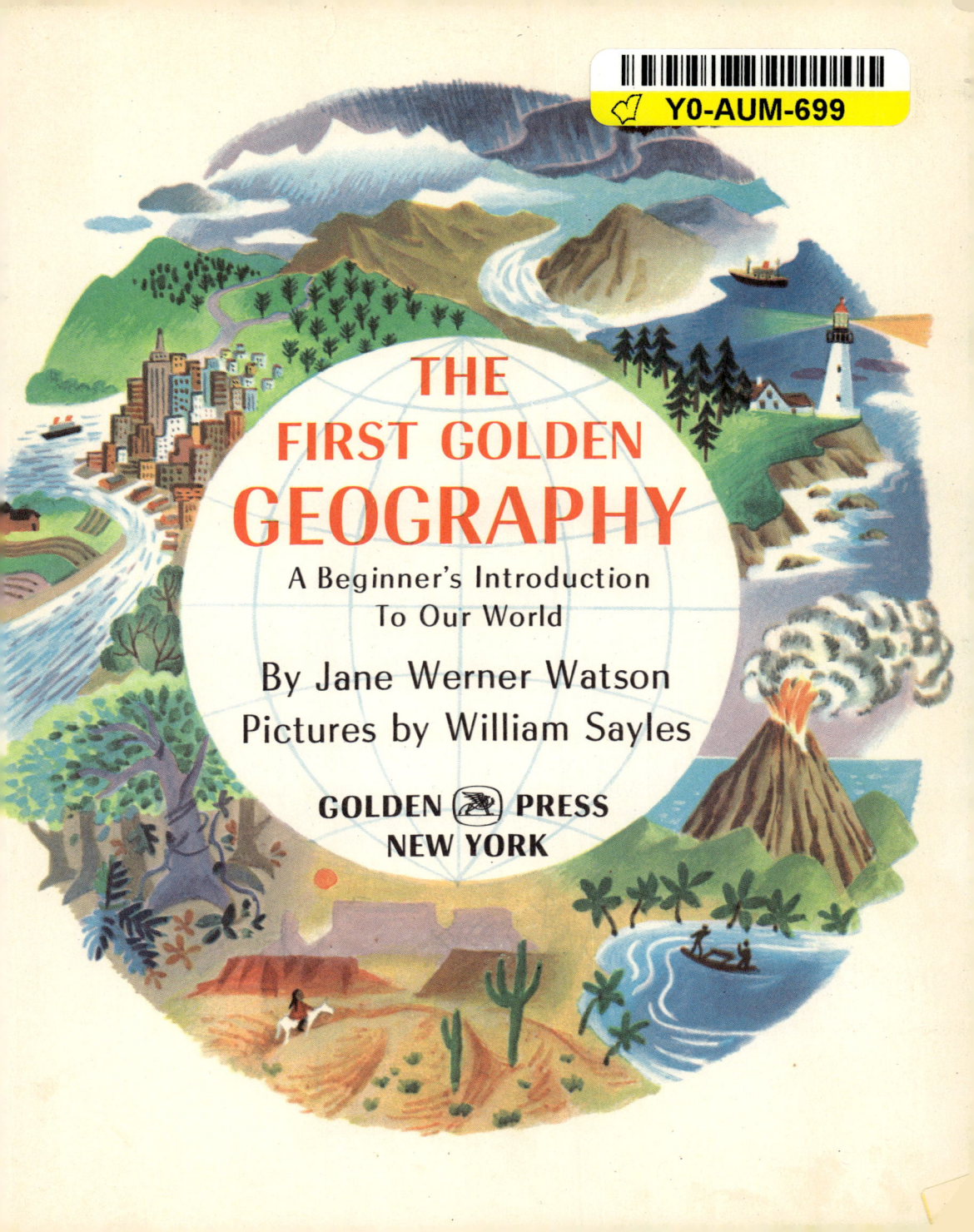

A Beginner's Introduction To Our World

By Jane Werner Watson
Pictures by William Sayles

GOLDEN PRESS · NEW YORK

THIS LITTLE GOLDEN BOOK WAS PREPARED UNDER THE SUPERVISION OF
MARY REED, Ph.D.

This Little Golden Book is a child's introduction to the world he lives in. It was written by Jane Werner Watson, who has written or planned many Golden Books. The pictures are by William Sayles.

© Copyright 1955 by Golden Press, Inc. All rights reserved, including the right of reproduction in whole or in part in any form. Designed and produced by Artists and Writers Press, Inc. Printed in the U.S.A. by Western Printing and Lithographing Company. Published by Golden Press, Inc., New York. Published simultaneously in Canada by The Musson Book Company, Ltd., Toronto

Our earth is round.
It is a huge, round ball.
It moves forever through space.

We cannot see the roundness,
standing here on earth.
The earth is too big for that.
Even high up in an airplane
we only see it curve a little
far, far away.

Perhaps from way out in space
we might look back and see our earth
round as a ball,
in its blanket of air.
 But standing here on earth
there is plenty we can see.

We can see mountains, great high mountains, pushed up into rocky peaks.

Some of the mountains are so tall they always have snow on top.

Some of the mountains have rivers of ice called glaciers,
moving slowly, slowly down their slopes.
When the ice reaches warmer, lower slopes,
it melts into small trickling streams.
Or the glacier may move slowly into the ocean.
Then big chunks of ice break off into the water.
They are called icebergs,
and they float away.

Some mountains spit out smoke and fire,
and even melted rocks.

The melted rocks bubble up
from the earth's center.

These mountains are called volcanoes.

We can see mountains
in long lines called ranges,
with their points called peaks,
sometimes higher than the clouds.
And we can see lower, rounded hills.

Between the mountains or the hills
we see the valleys, the lower land.
Along the valleys, rivers often run.
Some rivers start from melting snow
up in the mountains, high above.

The rivers run downhill, always downhill,
joining other rivers and growing larger.
They move always toward some ocean or sea.
  We can see rivers,
slow old rivers,
running slowly down wide, shallow valleys.

We can see swifter, wilder rivers
that have cut down through rock beds.
After long ages the river runs along
at the bottom of a steep-sided canyon
it has cut.

We can see the shore of the ocean or sea
that the rivers run into.
The shore may be flat and sandy.
It may be rocky and steep,
with high cliffs the waves tear at every day.

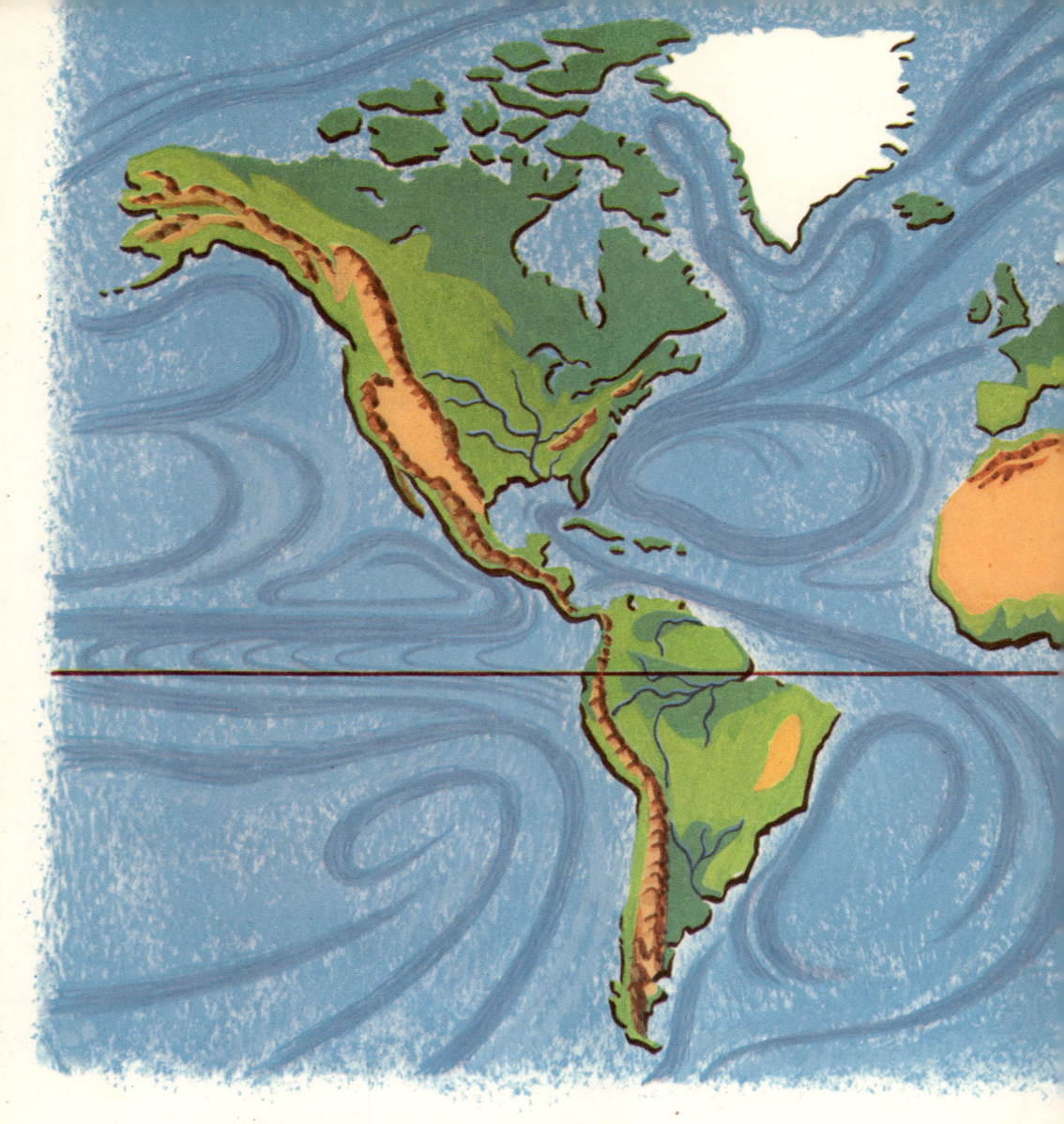

We can never see all of an ocean or sea from the shore or even from a boat because the seas and oceans are too big.

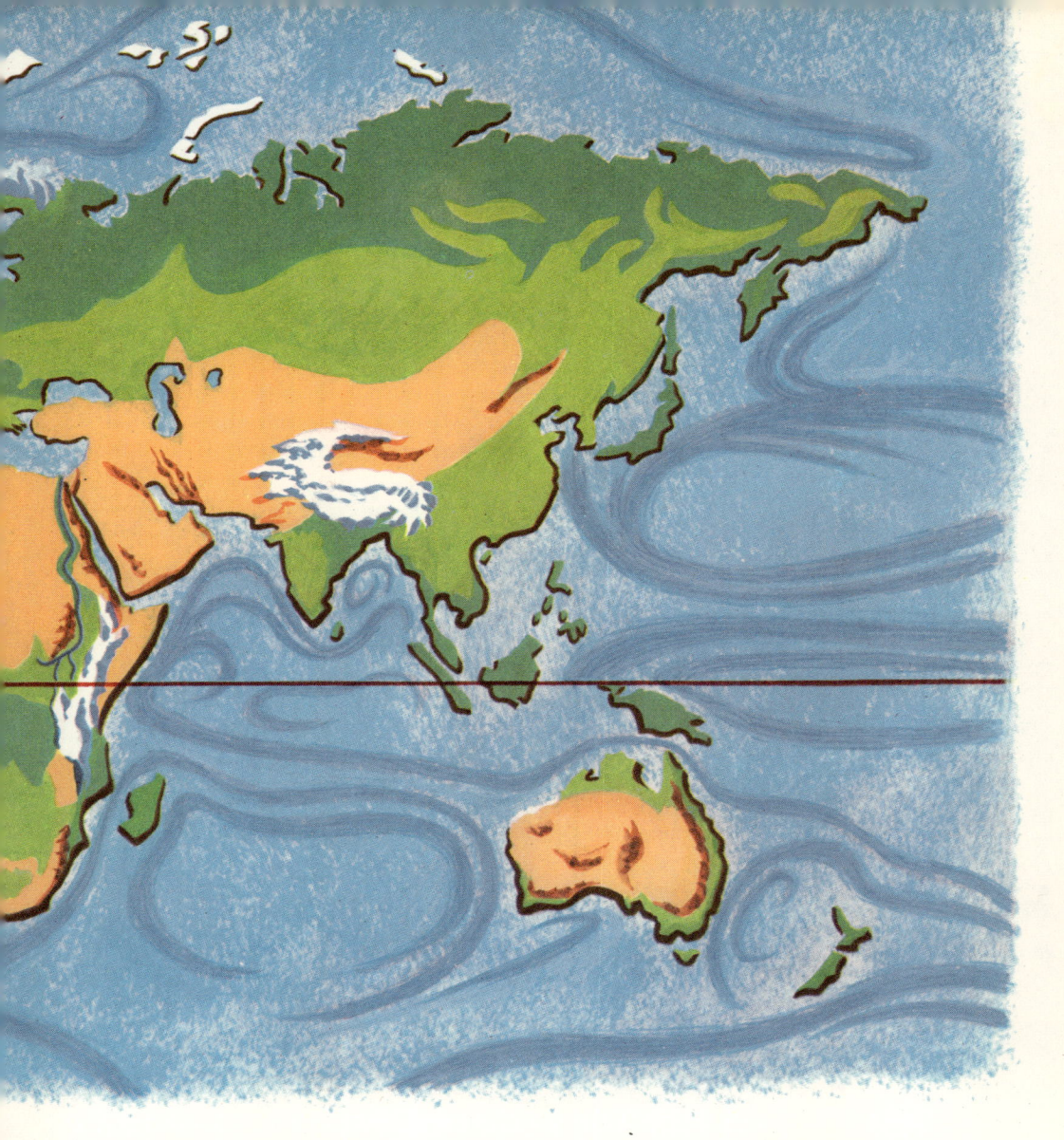

The oceans flow together all around the earth,
in a great blanket of water,
with land poking up through it.

The small pieces of land
with water all around them
are called islands.

Small bodies of water
with land all around them
are called lakes or ponds.

The huge stretches of land around the seas are called continents.

North America is one continent.

It has mountain ranges.

It has great rivers and valleys.

It has high grassy plains called prairies.

It has low grassy marshes, and watery swamps.

Where it is too cold for trees to grow,
and too cold for most animals,
there are frozen plains called tundras.

Where it is hot, and rains almost every day,
there are jungles.
The trees and vines and flowers
grow and grow until they hide the sky.

Some other places it seldom rains.
Then there is a desert.
The ground is powdery, sandy dry.
The winds sweep up loose grains of sand.
They move huge sand dunes,
grain by grain.

The sands blown by the wind polish rocks.
They cut chunks of rock
into arches and spires, mesas and buttes,
by rubbing away the softer parts.
The wind does that, with the help
of floods of water now and then.

There are so many different kinds of places
to see on our wonderful earth—
cities and wilderness, hot places and cold!
And we can explore and visit them all
some day soon, when you grow up.